MINDFUL MASTERY: A GUIDE TO PEACE AND PRESENCE

MINDFUL MASTERY: A GUIDE TO PEACE AND PRESENCE

KIMBERLY ACOSTA

Kimberly Acosta
Mindful Mastery: A Guide to Peace and Presence

Published by Spines Publishing Platform
ISBN: 979-8-89569-728-3

CONTENTS

INTRODUCTION

Welcome to *Mindful Mastery: A Guide to Peace and Presence*! In this ebook, we will explore the powerful practices of mindfulness and meditation and how they can transform your life in profound ways.

Mindfulness is the practice of being fully present and engaged in the moment, without judgment or attachment to particular outcomes. It involves paying attention to your thoughts, feelings, physical sensations, and the environment around you with curiosity and openness. By developing this awareness, you can cultivate a sense of peace, clarity, and balance in your daily life.

Meditation, on the other hand, is a formal practice that involves focusing your attention on a particular object, such as your breath, a mantra, or a visualization. Through regular meditation sessions, you can train your mind to be more focused, calm, and resilient in the face of challenges.

The benefits of incorporating mindfulness and meditation into your daily life are numerous. Research has shown that these practices can reduce stress, anxiety, and depression; improve focus, creativity, and memory; enhance emotional regulation; and foster a greater sense of overall well-being and happiness.

By tuning into the present moment and quieting the mind through mindfulness and meditation, you can develop greater self-awareness, compassion, and connection to yourself and others. These practices can help you navigate the ups and downs of life with more grace and resilience, allowing you to live more fully and authentically.

In the following chapters, we will delve deeper into the principles and techniques of mindfulness and meditation, offering practical exercises and guidance to help you integrate these practices into your daily routine. Whether you are new to these practices or have been exploring them for some time, this ebook will provide you with valuable tools and insights to deepen your understanding and experience of mindfulness and meditation.

So, come along on this journey of self-discovery and transformation as we explore "Mindful Mastery" together. May you find peace, stillness, and presence in the midst of life's chaos and challenges.

1

UNDERSTANDING MINDFULNESS

In today's fast-paced and stressful world, practicing mindfulness has become increasingly popular as a way to cope with the challenges of daily life. But what exactly is mindfulness, and how can it benefit our mental health? In this chapter, we will explore the definition of mindfulness, its history, the science behind it, and how it can be incorporated into our daily lives.

What is mindfulness?

Mindfulness can be defined as the act of paying attention to the present moment, without judgment or attachment to the past or future. It involves being fully aware of our thoughts, feelings, sensations, and surroundings in a non-reactive manner. By practicing mindfulness, we can cultivate a sense of inner peace and calm, even in the midst of chaos.

In the realm of psychological well-being, mindfulness is frequently used as a therapeutic approach to reduce stress, anxiety, and depression. Research has demonstrated its effectiveness in enhancing emotional regulation and improving overall mental health (Keng et al., 2011; Goyal et al., 2014).

The History of Mindfulness

This summary highlights the evolution of mindfulness and its ancient roots, emphasizing its significance in both spiritual and clinical contexts.

Mindfulness has its roots in ancient Eastern philosophies, particularly in Buddhist meditation practices. The concept of mindfulness was first introduced to the medical community by Jon Kabat-Zinn, who defines mindfulness as "paying attention in a particular way: on purpose, in the present moment, and non-judgmentally" (Kabat-Zinn, 1990). Since then, mindfulness has gained widespread popularity and is used widely in therapeutic settings to improve mental well-being.

Mindfulness, or "sati," is an essential component of Buddhist teachings that dates back to the 6th century BCE. It emphasizes awareness of the present moment, thoughts, feelings, and bodily sensations. In Hindu practices such as those found in the Yoga Sutras, along with similar concepts in Taoism, stress living in harmony with the present moment (Eliade, 1987).

"Meditation in ancient India spread across Asia, adapting to different cultural contexts" (Chopra & Simon, 1994), and Alan Watts popularized Zen and mindfulness concepts in Western culture (Watts, 1957).

In the early 20th century, the introduction of Eastern philosophies gained popularity in the West, leading to various mindfulness books, apps, and programs. It became a tool used in schools and corporate settings.

Today, mindfulness is practiced globally, embraced for its health benefits, personal development, and well-being. It has also been integrated into psychology, with mindfulness-based cognitive therapy (MBCT) among other approaches further validating its efficacy.

How Mindfulness Affects the Brain

Neuroimaging, in recent studies, have shown how mindfulness has an effect on the brain. Regularly practicing mindfulness can lead to functional and structural changes in the brain regions that have a direct correlation with emotional regulations and executive function.

The Prefrontal Cortex, Amygdala and Hippocampus are directly effected by mindfulness.

The prefrontal cortex, the area of the brain that is responsible for decision-making, self-control, and attention, showed an increase in thickness and activity in individuals who practiced mindfulness on a regular basis (Davidson et al., 2003). When this area of the brain is enhanced, it shows improvements in emotional regulation and cognitive function.

The amygdala plays an important role in processing emotions and stress responses. Studies have shown that individuals who practiced mindfulness and underwent neuroimaging studies showed a decrease in activity in the amygdala area of their brains. The reduction is associated with lower stress levels related to fear and anxiety, which suggests that the practice of mindfulness can mitigate the effects of stress (Desbordes et al., 2012).

The Hippocampus is responsible for memory and learning and is directly affected by mindfulness. Studies have shown that regularly practicing mindfulness can increase grey matter density in this region, which is linked to emotional resilience and improved memory (Hillel et al., 2011).

Numerous studies have shown that practicing mindfulness can have a positive impact on mental health. Mindfulness has been found to reduce stress, anxiety, and depression, and to improve overall well-being. It has also been shown to enhance focus, attention, and emotional regulation. The science behind mindfulness shows that mindfulness has the ability to rewire the brain, creating new neural pathways that promote a state of relaxation and awareness.

"Mindfulness Benefits: Physical and Mental Health"

By incorporating mindfulness into our daily lives, we can improve our mental health in numerous ways. Mindfulness helps us become aware of our thoughts and emotions, allowing us to respond to them in a constructive manner. It can also help us break free from negative thought patterns and cultivate a positive mindset. Overall, mindfulness can help us live with greater ease and resilience, even in the face of life's challenges.

The psychological benefits of mindfulness are well documented, making it a great tool for mental health and clinical psychology treatments. Many treatments available incorporate mindfulness to reduce stress, anxiety, and enhance emotional regulation.

Stress reduction has shown promising results for eliminating symptoms of anxiety and depression. A systematic review by Goyal et al. (2014) indicated that mindfulness meditation can lead to moderate improvements in anxiety and depression compared to control conditions.

Research indicates that when an individual practices mindfulness, they can identify and manage emotional responses better, leading to improved interpersonal relationships and overall emotional health (Keng et al., 2011).

Mindfulness benefits extend further than mental health; it also plays a positive role in physical health. Some other health improvements include pain management, immune function, and cardiovascular health.

A meta-analysis by Veehof et al. (2016) concluded that mindfulness can lead to significant reductions in pain perception and improvements in the quality of life for individuals suffering from chronic pain conditions.

Mindfulness practice is also associated with lower blood pressure and improved cardiovascular health. A review by Joseph et al. (2016) highlighted the positive impact of mindfulness on heart health, particularly through stress reduction and improved emotional regulation.

The science behind the profound impact on both mental and physical health associated with mindfulness has been shown to be positive. As research continues to evolve, individuals can better appreciate the transformative potential of mindfulness.

Incorporating Mindfulness

There are many different ways to incorporate mindfulness into our daily routine. Some popular practices include mindful meditation, mindful breathing, mindful body scan exercises, and mindful walking. Additionally, simple everyday activities such as eating, washing dishes, or even driving can be transformed into mindfulness practices by bringing our full attention to the present moment.

Start your day with intention. Before jumping out of bed and getting right to your morning hustle, take a few minutes to breathe deeply. Start your day by grounding yourself in the present by reflecting on what you are grateful for. Cultivating positive thoughts and feelings will set the tone for the rest of the day.

Incorporating mindfulness into your workday can enhance your focus and productivity. Focus on one task at a time. Take mindful breaks to step away, breathe, and stretch. When colleagues are talking to you, practice mindful listening by actively listening without interruptions, allowing them to express their thoughts.

When you are driving or commuting, pay attention to your surroundings. Take in the sounds and smells without distractions. When you find yourself waiting in lines or at a light, take that time to breathe and center yourself.

Before you go to bed, practice taking a digital detox to clear your mind. Write about your day, focusing on challenges, joys, and gratitude. Engage in reading, meditation, and stretching before bed, allowing the transition to flow flawlessly.

In conclusion, understanding mindfulness is the first step toward harnessing its benefits for our mental health and well-being. By taking the time to cultivate mindfulness in our daily lives, we can experience greater peace, joy, and clarity in our minds. So why not give it a try and see how mindfulness can transform your life?

2

THE PRACTICE OF MEDITATION

What is Meditation?

Meditation is a practice that has been around for thousands of years, with roots in various spiritual and philosophical traditions. It is a mental exercise that involves focusing the mind on a particular object, thought, or activity to achieve a state of clarity, awareness, and inner peace. The ultimate goal of meditation is to attain a deeper understanding of oneself and the world around us.

Different Types of Meditation Practices

There are many different types of meditation practices, each with its own unique focus and technique. Some of the most popular forms of meditation establish a sense of goodwill toward oneself and others, cultivate compassion, encourage being present without judgment, promote relaxation, and enhance awareness of physical sensations.

Mental and Physical Wellness and Meditation

Its been well-documented that meditation benefits both physical and mental wellness. Regular practice of mediation has shown to reduce stress, depression, and anxiety, enhance well-being, improve concentration and focus, heighten self awareness and emotional regulation. Meditation also has positive effects on physical health, as it is known to have an effect on lowering blood pressure, boosting immune responses and improve sleep.

Establishing a Regular Meditation Routine

Making meditation a part of your daily routine can be challenging, but with dedication and commitment, it is possible. To get started, I have provided some tips:

1. Find a comfortable space free of distractions where you can meditate.
2. Plan a specific time each day to practice meditation.
3. Start slow with just a few minutes a day and gradually increase how long you meditate as you become comfortable.
4. Try different kinds of meditation to see what suits you best.
5. Show yourself patience, as new skills take time to develop.

Meditation and Common Problems

Although meditation has many benefits, it is common to face challenges when embarking on the journey. One might find themselves having difficulty focusing, experiencing feelings of frustration or self-doubt, restlessness, or wanting to do something else while in the act of meditating. Overcoming these challenges will require you to approach meditation with an open mind. It is normal to have ups and downs because meditation is a practice. Patience and persistence are key to experiencing the transformation mediation can bring to your life.

3

THE CONNECTION BETWEEN MINDFULNESS AND MEDITATION

Often seen as two separate practices, mindfulness and meditation are connected and complement each other. When combined, they can have a powerful impact on emotional, physical, and mental well-being.

The Role of Mindfulness in Enhancing Meditation Practice

Mindfulness involves the practice of being aware and present in the moment, without judgment. When we incorporate mindfulness into our lives, we can develop the ability to observe our emotions and thoughts without allowing them to control our actions. It's essential to be aware of our thoughts and emotions in order to practice meditation and stay focused and centered during meditation practices to gain a deep experience.

How Meditation Can Deepen Mindfulness

In order to cultivate a sense of inner calm and quiet our minds, we have to practice mindfulness. This creates an ideal condition for meditation and getting into a deep state of relaxation and concentration. Being mindful will help prevent our minds from wandering and getting lost in distractions.

Mindfulness has the ability to cultivate a feeling of inner peace. When you practice focusing on the present, you can experience a reduction in stress and anxiety during your practice and afterward.

Since meditation and mindfulness are often linked together, it is important to know how meditation plays a role in mindfulness. Meditation helps to enhance mindfulness practices by deepening our experience. The meditation practice cultivates a sense of inner stillness and focus that can be carried into our daily lives. The awareness cultivated from practice allows us to stay attentive and present in all situations and leads to emotional resilience, clarity, and focus.

In turn, when you practice meditation, you develop a sense of compassion and kindness toward yourself and others. These qualities can deepen the connection to the present moment and cultivate a positive and open attitude toward life.

Techniques for Integrating Mindfulness and Meditation Daily

Integrating meditation and mindfulness into your daily life involves setting aside a few minutes each day to practice meditation. You will need a quiet space where you can get comfortable and focus on your breathing or a mantra you choose. While meditating, you should focus on your thoughts and sensations without judgment.

Once you start practicing meditation, you should also try to incorporate mindfulness into your daily life. Practice being present in every moment as your day goes on. You can practice this while you are eating, talking, or walking. By incorporating mindfulness into each moment of your day, you will cultivate a sense of peace, presence, and awareness in your daily life.

Mindfulness and meditation are powerful practices that can enhance each other and help deepen the connection to the present moment. Combining the two practices can cultivate a greater sense of compassion, clarity, and peace in our lives. Once you start incorporating these practices into your daily life, you will see the transformation in your body, mind, and spirit.

1. Create a mindful environment: Find a calm space free from distractions.
2. Establish a Routine: We all know consistency is key, but when you integrate meditation and mindfulness into your daily routine, they will soon become habits.
3. Reflect on your practice: Self-awareness fosters understanding and growth. So, if you reflect on your experience, you can consider what worked well and what could be improved after your sessions.

Some techniques you can employ in your daily life might include the following practices:

- Gratitude Practice: Creating a positive emotional state provides a sense of peace. Integrate gratitude into your meditation.
- "Loving-Kindness Meditation: Send positive and loving thoughts and wishes not only toward yourself but also to others. This creates feelings of love and compassion."
- Mindful Visualization: Picture yourself in a serene, calm place. This cultivates a sense of calm and refuge from your daily life.

Mindfulness is essential during meditation, as it enriches and transforms your experience. You can enhance focus, deepen emotional awareness, and foster peace. When you incorporate mindfulness into your meditation, you can guide yourself toward a profound connection to yourself and the world around you. Mindfulness can elevate your meditation practice to new heights.

When you incorporate emotional processing in meditation, the first step is to observe your emotions. Pay attention to when emotions rise to the surface, and instead of pushing them away, observe them without attachment. Being compassionate with yourself increases the benefits of the meditation practice, allowing for understanding and emotional release.

> "Compassionate reflection can be incorporated when difficult emotions arise. When this occurs, remind yourself that it's okay to feel what you are feeling. Having some compassion for yourself allows space for healing and growth."

4

CULTIVATING MINDFULNESS AND MEDITATION IN DAILY LIFE

We live in a fast-paced world, and it is very easy to get caught up in chaos. We are faced with juggling work responsibilities, managing personal relationships, and managing our family responsibilities; it's no wonder we encounter frustrations and stress. When we cultivate mindfulness and incorporate meditation into our daily practice, we can find a sense of balance and peace despite the chaos.

One way to incorporate mindfulness into your daily life is by "mindful eating." This involves being aware of what you are consuming, as well as the sensations and feelings that arise while consuming your food. You can develop a deeper appreciation for the nourishment the food provides and listen to your body's hunger cues.

Another way you can incorporate mindfulness into your daily life is by paying attention to how you communicate with others. How you communicate has a profound impact on your relationships. Are you fully present and attentive while communicating with others? In order to improve the quality of your relationships and build a sense of connection with those around you, you have to engage in conversation and be present. Mindful communication involves understanding what is being said, speaking with intention, listening actively and practicing empathy.

Many of us wake up and hit the ground running. Do you pay attention to your body when you are moving? When you slow down and become mindful of your body, you feel more relaxed and connected to yourself. The next time you go for a walk, pay attention to your breathing and the way your body feels; cultivate a sense of calm and presence. When you do physical activities like yoga, meditation or walking you are not only working on your physical health and flexibility but you are also reducing stress and anxiety.

- Practice mindfulness exercises.
- Eat mindfully
- Walk slowly
- Take a break.
- Practice gratitude
- "Slow down your movements."
- Practice martial arts.
- "Cultivate a healthy environment."

Incorporating the practices we discussed into your daily life will involve setting aside time each day. You can start with short breathing exercises, or you can practice mindfulness while you are completing household chores.

When you cultivate mindfulness and incorporate meditation into your daily life, it can have a profound impact on your overall happiness. When you practice mindful communication, eating, movement, and meditation, you are learning to be present and fully engage in each moment, thus finding a sense of balance and peace amidst the chaos that so many of us face in our daily lives.

In conclusion, incorporating meditation and cultivating mindfulness in your daily life can have a profound impact on your overall happiness and well-being.

5

ADVANCED PRACTICES AND RESOURCES

In this chapter, we will explore practices and provide resources that will guide you on your mindfulness and meditation journey. The tools and techniques provided will enhance your practice and unlock even more profound benefits.

I have listed some popular meditation techniques and provided some guides. You can pick and choose which are your favorites. I suggest trying them all and implementing the ones that you enjoy the most into your daily life. You can switch them up daily to get the most out of your practice.

My favorite five techniques are:

- "Counting your breath."
- "Visualization" or guided imagery.
- Mindful walking.
- Belly Breathing
- Trataka
- "Body Scan Meditation"
- Chakra Meditation
- Spiritual meditation
- Music meditation
- Yoga

There are many choices available to you, so find one that fits your lifestyle and that you enjoy doing. Let's dive into some of my favorites.

Counting your breath

1. Get into a comfortable position and start taking long, slow, deep breaths.
2. "Breathe in through your nose and out through your mouth."
3. Focus all of your attention on your breath and count slowly to 100 (breathing in is 1, and breathing out is 2, etc.).
4. If your mind lingers, bring your attention back to your breathing and start from where you left off.
5. Continue until you get to one hundred.

This breath work helps to calm both mind and body by bringing the nervous system into a state of peace. The next time you feel like you are in a state of "fight or flight," try to count your breaths to bring yourself into a more controlled state.

Visual or guided imagery

1. Smell flowers
2. "Watch the waves hit the shore."
3. Imagine a peaceful place in your mind; add to it.
4. See or visualize a bird chirping or a flock of birds chirping.
5. Visualize a tranquil lake at sunrise or sunset.

This is a focused practice that uses all five of your senses and ignites positive messages throughout your body. This can be done in real time, or it can be done with your imagination. This practice helps put you in a relaxed state and can be done anywhere at any time! It's a really great practice to reduce stress and increase well-being.

Mindful Walking

1. Choose a foot to start with.
2. "Walk with intention."
3. "Focus on your footing; feel your feet hitting the ground with each step."
4. Notice when your thoughts take over; focus back on your footing and stay grounded.
5. Connect with the sounds, smells, and beauty surrounding you.

6. Let yourself aimlessly walk and take in the different surroundings you may encounter.

Mindful walking can help reduce anxiety and improve mood. It can create a sense of awe and positive emotions. Among those amazing benefits, it can also help with sleep and get your blood flowing.

Belly Breathing

1. Sit in a comfortable chair or lie down.
2. "Put one hand on your belly and the other on your chest."
3. "Breathe in slowly through your nose."
4. When you are breathing in, push your stomach out as far as you can. The hand placed on your belly should move, but not the one on your chest.
5. "Breathe out through your mouth; you should feel the hand on your belly move in."
6. Do this for ten minutes a few times a day, if you can.

This technique helps to slow down your breathing so you can catch your breath and use less energy to breathe. This breathing technique helps to lower blood pressure, stress levels, and other critical body functions. It has also been linked to helping with GERD, acid reflux, and chronic cough by strengthening the diaphragm.

Trataka

1. Choose a comfortable position.
2. Light a candle and place it at eye level, two feet in front of you.
3. Place your hands on either your legs or stomach (whichever is comfortable for you).
4. Close your eyes and take ten deep breaths through your nose (inhale for the count of 3 and exhale for the count of 6). Allow yourself to be in the moment.
5. Open your eyes and immediately focus on the candle flame right at the tip of the wick (where the flame is the brightest and strongest).
6. Do not blink; watch it even if your eyes start to burn and water.
7. When you cannot keep your eyes open any longer, relax the muscles that worked so hard to keep them open and close your eyes while keeping the image of the flame in your mind.
8. When the image fades, you are done.

This meditation practice helps to improve sleep, clarity, and concentration; supports eye health; and reduces stress, anxiety, and racing thoughts.

Body Scan Meditation

1. Get comfortable (lying down, preferably).
2. Take a few deep breaths (slow breaths from your belly).
3. Bring attention to your feet.

4. "Breathe into the tension. If you notice uncomfortable sensations, focus your attention on them and breathe into them; you should feel the tension leaving your body with your breath."
5. Scan your entire body (move from your feet all the way up to the top of your head; you will notice where you are holding your stress. Continue to breathe into the areas where you feel the most tension).

This meditation helps rebuild your connection to being in the moment. Instead of worrying about the future or the past, it forces you to be present. This practice helps with better sleep, pain relief, emotional regulation, and increased self-awareness.

Mindfulness and Meditation Retreats.

Attending a mindfulness or meditation retreat can truly immerse you in a focused environment of self-awareness, inner stillness, and personal reflection. It provides space to:

1. Deepen your connection to the present moment.
2. Cultivate mental clarity and emotional balance.
3. Experience a heightened sense of inner calm.
4. Engage in sustained, uninterrupted practice of mindfulness techniques.
5. Foster self-discovery and introspection.
6. Detach from everyday distractions, allowing for a deeper connection to your inner self.
7. Explore a sense of connection to nature, others, or a higher consciousness.

Mindfulness and Meditation Apps and Websites

There is an abundant variety of apps and websites available that offer free guided meditations and mindfulness exercises. These tools can provide guidance for you on your journey toward incorporating mindfulness and meditation into your daily life. Some apps include Headspace, Calm, Smiling Mind, The Mindfulness app, Ten Percent and Insight Timer. YouTube also provides tons of free videos.

Recommended Books on Mindfulness and Meditation

There are many excellent books on mindfulness and meditation that can deepen your understanding of these practices and provide guidance for your journey. Some recommended titles include

- "Wherever You Go, There You Are" by Jon Kabat-Zinn,
- "You Become What You Think" by Shubham Kumar Singh,
- "The Art of Living" by Thich Nhat Hanh,
- "The Mindful Body" by Ellen J. Langer,
- "The Zen Monkey and the Lotus Flower" by Tenpa Yeshe, and
- "The Power of Now" by Eckhart Tolle.

Tips for Maintaining Mindfulness and Meditation Practice

Building a mindfulness and meditation practice requires dedication, patience, and consistency. Here are some tips to help you maintain a sustainable practice:

- Set aside time each day to practice. To start, you just need a few minutes.
- Experiment with different techniques.
- Be gentle with yourself if you miss a session.
- Find a community with others who practice or a teacher to help guide you on your journey.
- Continue to explore and learn about mindfulness and meditation.

6

BENEFITS OF MINDFULNESS AND MEDITATION

By incorporating these practices and utilizing the resources provided into your mindfulness and meditation practice, you can enhance your journey and foster a heightened sense of awareness, presence, and inner tranquility.

As we wrap up our journey of integrating mindfulness and meditation into our daily routines, let's take a moment to reflect on our progress and growth. We've learned to foster a deeper sense of awareness, presence, and inner peace, which has contributed to a more balanced and fulfilling life.

It's important to recognize the effort and commitment involved in this practice. Staying dedicated to mindfulness and meditation can be challenging amid the busyness and chaos of daily life. Nonetheless, the benefits of these practices far outweigh the time and energy spent. It is essential to acknowledge the efforts and dedication that have been put into this practice. It is not always easy to commit to these practices daily. However, the benefits that come from these practices are well worth the time and energy invested.

Keep in mind that mindfulness and meditation are not just strategies for dealing with stress; they are a way of life to be embraced daily. By nurturing a sense of presence and awareness, you'll be better prepared to face the challenges that arise in your busy lives.

In closing, I want to highlight the transformative potential of mindfulness and meditation. These practices can significantly enhance our lives, leading us to greater peace, happiness, and fulfillment. As you move forward, I encourage you to appreciate the beauty of the present moment and to approach each day with mindfulness and gratitude.

Thank you for joining me on this exploration of mindfulness and meditation. I hope this journey has been enriching and enlightening for you, and that you continue to delve deeper into these practices in the years ahead. Wishing you peace, joy, and fulfillment on your mindfulness journey.

7

THE APPENDIX

In this final chapter of the ebook, you will find additional resources to assist you on your journey of self-discovery.

Guided Meditation Scripts: If you are seeking a moment of calm and clarity, we have included a selection of guided meditation scripts to help you center yourself and find peace in the present moment. These scripts can be used as a tool for relaxation, stress relief, and mindfulness practice.

Loving-Kindness Meditation

- Find a comfortable place to sit, close your eyes, and take a few deep breaths. Allow your body to relax.
- Repeat phrases to yourself, such as "May I be well, happy, and peaceful," "May I be free from suffering," and "May I be healthy, safe, and strong."
- Visualize a loved one and repeat: "May you be well, happy, and peaceful. May you be free from suffering. May you be healthy, safe, and strong."

- Next, think of an individual; it could be a friend, an acquaintance, or someone whom you find challenging. Repeat the phrases for each.
- Finally, expand your wishes to everyone around the world: "May everyone be happy, healthy, peaceful, and free from suffering."
- When that mediation is complete, take a moment to feel the warmth of your wishes, then gently open your eyes.

Guided Visualization: Safe Place

- Get comfortable (sitting or lying down) and close your eyes. Take a few deep breaths.
- Imagine a place where you feel completely safe and at peace. This could be a beach, a forest, or any place that brings you comfort.
- Visualize all the colors, sounds, and smells. What do you see? What do you hear? Take in the details.
- Allow the feelings of comfort and safety to surround you. Imagine these feelings growing stronger with each breath.
- Spend a few moments enjoying this space you created. When you're ready, slowly bring your awareness back to the present and open your eyes.

Gratitude Meditation

- Find a comfortable position and close your eyes. Take a few deep breaths, allowing your body to relax.
- Think of three things for which you are grateful.

- Visualize each of these things in detail. What do they look like? How do they make you feel?
- Allow the feelings of gratitude to fill your heart and spread to every part of your body. Notice how this feeling changes your state of mind.
- Take a few more deep breaths, feeling this warmth, and when you're ready, gently open your eyes.

Breath Awareness Meditation

- Find a comfortable seated position. Allow your body to relax. Gently close your eyes.
- Take a deep breath in through your nose, filling your lungs completely. Hold for a moment, then exhale slowly through your mouth. Feel the tension release with each breath out.
- Next, allow your breath to return to its natural rhythm. Notice the sensation of air entering and leaving your nose. Observe the rise and fall of your chest or abdomen.
- If thoughts arise, acknowledge them without judgment and gently return your focus to your breath.
- Take a few more deep breaths, and then, when you are ready, slowly open your eyes.

Reflection Journal Prompts: Self-reflection is a powerful practice that can aid in personal growth and development. In this section, you will find a variety of journal prompts designed to inspire introspection and a deeper understanding of your thoughts, feelings, and experiences. Use these prompts as a starting point for reflection and journaling to gain insight into your innermost thoughts and emotions.

Reflection Journal Prompts

1. **Daily Gratitude**
    - Write down three or more things that you are grateful for today. How did they impact your day?
2. **Personal Growth**
    - Consider a recent challenge you've faced. What did you learn from it, and how did it help you grow?
3. **Values and Beliefs**
    - What principles are most important to you? How do they influence your decisions and actions?
4. **Mindfulness Experience**
    - Share a time when you felt completely engaged in the moment. What were you doing, and how did it feel?
5. **Future Aspirations**
    - Envision your life five years down the line. What do you hope to have achieved, and what steps can you take now to get there?
6. **Emotional Awareness**
    - Think about a strong emotion you experienced recently. What caused it, and how did you respond?
7. **Relationships**
    - Reflect on a meaningful relationship in your life. What makes it special, and how can you nurture it further?

8. **Self-Compassion**
    - Compose a letter to yourself from a challenging period, expressing compassion and empathy. What would you say?
9. **Life Lessons**
    - Remember a significant life lesson you've learned. How has it impacted who you are today?
10. **Creative Expression**
    - What are some things that make you feel creative and alive? How can you incorporate more of them into your life?

We hope that this appendix serves as a valuable resource for you on your journey of self-discovery and personal growth. May you continue to explore, learn, and evolve as you navigate the path toward a more fulfilling and meaningful life.

BIBLIOGRAPHY

- Kabat-Zinn, J. (1990). *Full Catastrophe Living: Using the Wisdom of Your Body and Mind to Face Stress, Pain, and Illness*. Delta.
- Bodhi, B. (2000). *The Connected Discourses of the Buddha: A New Translation of the Samyutta Nikaya*. Wisdom Publications. Davidson, R. J., Sheridan, J. F., & Kolles, L. (2003). "The Functional Neuroanatomy of Emotion Regulation: A Perspective from affective neuroscience." Emotion, 3(2), 144-174.
- Eliade, M. (1987). *Yoga: Immortality and Freedom*. Princeton University Press. Desbordes, G., Negi, S., Pace, T. W., et al. (2012). "Effects of mindful meditation on emotional regulation in social anxiety disorder." Social Cognitive and Affective Neuroscience, 7(3), 243-250.
- Hölzel, B. K., Carmody, J., Vangel, M., et al. (2011). "Mindfulness practice leads to increases in regional brain gray matter density." Psychiatry Research: Neuroimaging, 191(1), 36-43.
- Goyal, M., Singh, S., Sibinga, E. M. S., et al. (2014). "Meditation programs for psychological stress and well-being: A systematic review and meta-analysis." *JAMA Internal Medicine, 174*(3), 357-368.
- Keng, S. L., Smoski, M. J., & Robins, C. J. (2011). "Effects of mindfulness on psychological health: A review of empirical studies." Clinical Psychology Review*,, 31(6), 1041-1056.
- Joseph, N. T., Robinson, D. P., et al. (2016). "Mindfulness Interventions and Cardiovascular Risk: A Systematic Review." *Journal of Clinical Hypertension, 18(1), 9-16.
- Keng, S. L., Smoski, M. J., & Robins, C. J. (2011). "Effects of mindfulness on psychological health: A review of empirical studies. Clinical Psychology Review*,, 31(6), 1041-1056.
- Chopra, D., & Simon, D. (1994). *The Seven Spiritual Laws of Success*. Amber-Allen Publishing.
- Photographs by Pixels.com
- Photographs by Adobestock.com

www.ingramcontent.com/pod-product-compliance
Lightning Source LLC
LaVergne TN
LVHW040929150826
845672LV00007B/2268
9798895697283